The United States Goes West

by
Adam McClellan

Editorial Offices: Glenview, Illinois • Parsippany, New Jersey • New York, New York
Sales Offices: Needham, Massachusetts • Duluth, Georgia • Glenview, Illinois
Coppell, Texas • Ontario, California • Mesa, Arizona

ISBN: 0-328-13575-5

5 6 7 8 9 10 V0G1 14 13 12 11 10 09 08 07

A New Nation

In 1776, thirteen American colonies declared their **independence** from Great Britain. They fought the American Revolution against Great Britain, and in 1780 Great Britain surrendered. A new nation was born—the United States of America.

In 1783 a treaty gave the United States the thirteen colonies—now states—and other territory west to the Mississippi River. Great Britain kept its lands in Canada. Spain controlled most of the territory south and west of the United States. Part of the territory west from the Mississippi was called Louisiana.

This 1784 map shows the borders of the new nation.

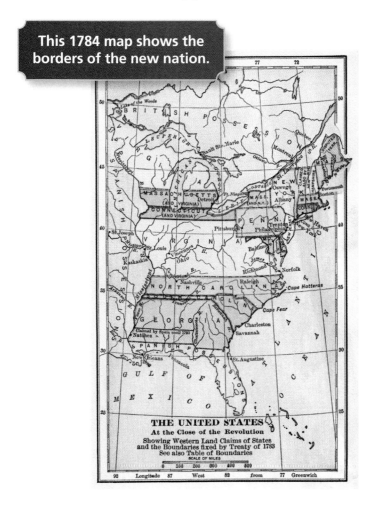

THE UNITED STATES
At the Close of the Revolution
Showing Western Land Claims of States
and the Boundaries fixed by Treaty of 1783
See also Table of Boundaries

When President Thomas Jefferson took office in 1801, he had a great interest in exploring lands to the west. He knew that the future of his country depended on control of this territory.

As long as Spain controlled the west, Jefferson was not worried. However, Spain's hold on its colonies seemed to be slowly slipping. Jefferson was sure that the United States could make a deal with Spain to gain Louisiana.

In 1802, Jefferson received shocking news. The Spanish had handed Louisiana over to the French! This changed everything. At the time, France was becoming the strongest country in Europe. If the French had plans for North America, it would be very hard for the United States to grow westward.

When Napoleon Bonaparte took control of France in 1799, he wanted to increase France's strength in North America. Taking over Spanish territory there gave France control of important ports.

Thomas Jefferson was greatly concerned when Spain handed Louisiana to the French. Suddenly, expanding westward became more difficult.

In 1803, James Monroe went to Paris to try to buy
New Orleans from the French. Jefferson told him,
". . . all hopes are fixed upon you. . . ."

The port of New Orleans in the early nineteenth century was an important trading and shipping center.

The Louisiana Purchase

French control of Louisiana gave Jefferson another worry: the Mississippi River. The United States and Spain agreed that American settlers could sell their goods in the important port of New Orleans.

No one knew what the French would do now that they controlled Louisiana. Jefferson feared that they would block American boats from using the port of New Orleans. This would cause damaging **economic** results.

With that in mind, Jefferson sent James Monroe to Paris to make a deal with the French. Monroe was to offer to buy New Orleans. The U.S. government would offer to pay almost nine and a half million dollars for the city.

When Monroe got to Paris on April 12, 1803, he was in for a surprise. Facing a possible war from England and other concerns, France was losing interest in controlling Louisiana. The day before Monroe arrived, the French government had made an offer to the U.S. agent in Paris. They said the United States could have all of Louisiana for the right price. Monroe and the agent signed a treaty agreeing to buy the entire Louisiana territory. The territory cost the United States only 15 million dollars.

The Louisiana Purchase doubled the size of the United States.

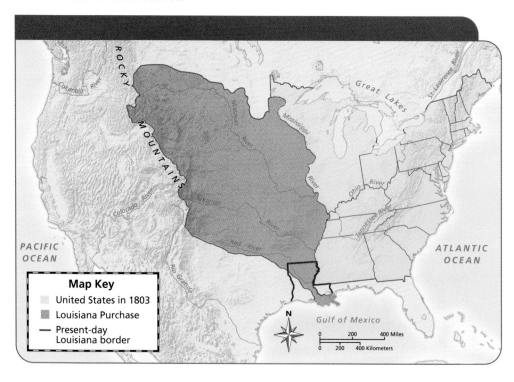

In 1793, Sir Alexander Mackenzie left his mark on a rock in Bella Coda, British Columbia, on the Canadian coast.

Sir Alexander Mackenzie

Exploring the New Lands

Jefferson had already made plans to explore the west. He wanted to find an easy water route to the Pacific Ocean. He was inspired by the explorations of Sir Alexander Mackenzie. In 1793, the Scottish fur trader had discovered a route through western Canada to the Pacific. Mackenzie's route was traveled almost all the way by boat. Jefferson hoped to keep British traders from gaining control of the fur trade near the Pacific Coast. He also was curious about the plants and animals in the lands west of the Mississippi.

Jefferson put together a small group named the Corps of Discovery. The group had about thirty men. The journey was to be led by two men who were already known for their skills in the wilderness: Meriwether Lewis and William Clark.

Jefferson had planned for the trip to take place no matter who owned the territory. Now, the Louisiana Purchase gave the explorers a new purpose. They would map out the country's new lands and make contact with Native Americans who made their homes there. Many of these people had never heard of the United States.

Members of the Corps of Discovery included skilled frontiersmen, hunters, woodcutters, and interpreters. They met with many groups of Native Americans.

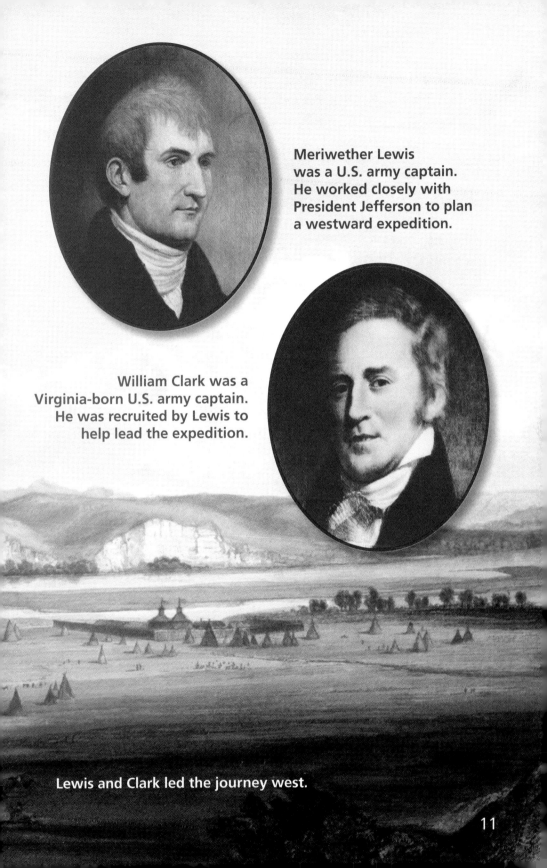

Meriwether Lewis
was a U.S. army captain.
He worked closely with
President Jefferson to plan
a westward expedition.

William Clark was a
Virginia-born U.S. army captain.
He was recruited by Lewis to
help lead the expedition.

Lewis and Clark led the journey west.

The explorers planned to follow the Missouri River as far west as they could and then find a way to the Pacific Ocean. In the fall of 1803, the Corps of Discovery arrived at St. Louis, on the Mississippi River near the point where the Missouri and Mississippi Rivers join. They spent the winter near there. They collected and sorted supplies and worked at becoming fit for the tough journey ahead. The following spring, the explorers **ventured** out.

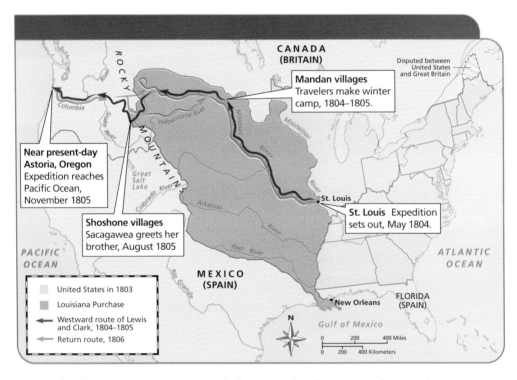

The journey west spanned thousands of miles. It began in St. Louis, on the Mississippi River, and led to the Pacific Ocean and back.

In early August, the explorers came across members of the Oto, a group of Native Americans. Lewis gave a speech explaining that the French and Spanish no longer ruled their land. They would now be part of the United States. The Oto leader thanked Lewis for his speech, and Lewis gave him gifts. The speech was repeated each time the explorers met a new group of Native Americans.

The Corps of Discovery met with many Native American leaders on their journey.

Near the end of October, the explorers came to a group of villages that belonged to the Mandan people. The villages were on the Great Bend of the Missouri River in what is now North Dakota. Here, they suffered the long winter. In his diary, Clark **scrawled** that the temperature was 45 degrees below

The expedition spent the winter at the Mandan villages along the Missouri River.

zero on a bitter December day. The Mandan gave the explorers a warm place to spend the winter.

The explorers made friendly contact with many Native Americans in the west, including the Shoshone, the Nez Perce, and the Walla Walla. They traded horses, food, and other supplies with these people.

In the summer of 1805, the explorers ran into a huge barrier, the Rocky Mountains. It took two months to cross the mountains and find another river to follow to the Pacific.

In November, they finally reached the Pacific Ocean. The team spent a cold, rainy winter in what is now Oregon. On March 23, 1806, they turned east and headed home.

The Louisiana Purchase was a big step toward making this country what it is today. It opened up new lands and erased a foreign power from the map of North America. The Lewis and Clark expedition inspired Americans to look west for their future. These key events in our history also came with problems.

The Corps of Discovery had to cross the rugged Bitterroot Range, which is part of the Rocky Mountains.

Settlers traveled up and down rivers
on flatboats loaded with freight.

Native Americans and the West

It didn't take long for people in the East to begin
moving west. On their return trip down the Missouri
River, Lewis and Clark met traders with boats loaded
with **freight**, hoping to trade with Native Americans
in the new territory.

As it turned out, however, Native Americans had
an uneasy relationship with the settlers.

The U.S. government promised land to Native Americans.

Many hoped that Native American tribes and settlers would coexist peacefully. Unfortunately, by the late 1820s, the government started a policy of keeping Native Americans separated from settlers. They did this by using land gained in the Louisiana Purchase.

Beginning in 1830, many tribes were forced off their homelands in the south. They were marched westward to a new "Indian Territory" west of the Mississippi River, in what is now Oklahoma. Areas such as this came to be called reservations.

This also affected the Native Americans already living in the territory. Settlers began moving into the area, but this land was not **vacant.** Native Americans lived and hunted there. As new settlements grew, Native Americans were forced from their homes.

The Native Americans packed up their homes.

Native Americans, forced to leave their lands in the east, made their long and difficult journey to the Indian Territory in Oklahoma.

This situation caused fighting between the new settlers and local Native Americans. To resolve the conflict, the government and Native American nations signed treaties setting aside certain lands for the settlers and other lands for the Native Americans.

The treaties promised that Native Americans would have their lands forever. This didn't happen. Instead, more settlers arrived to **overrun** the tribal lands, causing more conflict.

Within a hundred years of Lewis and Clark's expedition, the Native American groups these men had met were all forced onto reservations. The reservations made up only a small part of the lands on which they once lived. Jefferson's hopes for peace had died. Lewis and Clark unknowingly opened up the west for one group of people and closed it for another.

The choices Thomas Jefferson made in his first years as president forever changed the United States' shape, size, and history.

GRAND RUSH
FOR THE
INDIAN
TERRITORY!
Over 15,000,000 Acres ℔ Lan
NOW OPEN FOR SETTLEMENT !
Being part of the Land bought by the Governmen
1866 from the Indians for the Freedmen.
NOW IS THE CHANC
—TO—
PROCURE A HON
In this Beautiful Count
THE FINEST TIMBER !
THE RICHEST LAND !
THE FINEST WAT
WEST OF THE MISSISSIPPI RI
Every person over 21 years of age is entitled to 16
pre-emption or homestead, who wishes to settle in the In
estimated that over Fifty Thousand will move to this T
The Indians are rejoicing to have the

A pioneer family moves all of their belongings in a wagon going west.

Glossary

economic *adj.* related to money, business, and trade

freight *n.* transported goods

independence *n.* the condition of being free from the control of another country

overrun *v.* to spread through quickly

scrawled *v.* wrote quickly and sloppily

vacant *adj.* empty

ventured *n.* did something risky, often related to travel